Mediterranean Diet Cookbook

For Women Over 60

Senior Women's Guide to Eating and Living Well
with 50+ Delicious Recipes to Promote Healthy Aging

By

Rachel Carter

Copyright ©2024 by Rachel Cater

Table of Contents

INTRODUCTION

Meet Anita Johnson, a vibrant senior woman in her 60s who was determined to take control of her health as she embraced the golden years. Anita had always been active and independent, but she noticed her energy levels declining, and she struggled with occasional forgetfulness and extra weight that seemed to cling stubbornly despite her efforts. Concerned about her cognitive function, heart health, and overall well-being, Anita decided to make a change.

Inspired by the stories she read about the Mediterranean diet's health benefits, Anita embarked on a journey to revitalize her health. She started incorporating more fruits, vegetables, whole grains, and lean proteins into her meals while reducing her intake of processed foods and saturated fats. Anita was amazed at how delicious and satisfying

Mediterranean-inspired dishes could be, and she enjoyed experimenting with new recipes and flavors in her kitchen.

As weeks turned into months, Anita began to notice positive changes in her health. Her cognitive function improved, and she felt sharper and more focused than she had in years. Anita's heart health also benefited from her new dietary habits, as her cholesterol levels dropped, and her blood pressure normalized. Most importantly, Anita shed those extra pounds that had been weighing her down, and she felt lighter, stronger, and more confident in her skin. Thanks to the Mediterranean diet, Anita not only managed her health conditions that come with aging but also thrived. With each nutritious meal she enjoyed, Anita felt empowered and rejuvenated, ready to embrace all that life had to offer in her golden years.

CHAPTER ONE

What is the Mediterranean Diet?

The Mediterranean diet is a traditional eating pattern inspired by the culinary traditions of countries bordering the Mediterranean Sea, such as Greece, Italy, Spain, and Morocco. At its core, the Mediterranean diet emphasizes plant-based foods, including fruits, vegetables, whole grains, nuts, and legumes. Olive oil is the primary source of fat, used for cooking and dressing salads, while dairy products, such as cheese and yogurt, are consumed in moderation. Seafood and poultry are preferred sources of protein, with red meat eaten sparingly. Herbs and spices are used liberally to add flavor to dishes, while salt is used sparingly.

One of the defining characteristics of the Mediterranean diet is its emphasis on enjoying meals with family and friends. Meals are typically enjoyed slowly and savored, with an emphasis on fresh, seasonal ingredients. The Mediterranean diet is not just about what you eat but also how you eat, promoting a relaxed and social approach to dining.

Benefits of the Mediterranean Diet For Women Over 60

Heart Health: The Mediterranean diet is rich in heart-healthy fats, such as monounsaturated and polyunsaturated fats found in olive oil, nuts, and fatty fish. These fats help lower LDL cholesterol levels and reduce the risk of heart disease, heart attacks, and strokes.

Cognitive Function: Studies have shown that the Mediterranean diet is associated with improved cognitive function and a reduced risk of cognitive decline and dementia in older adults. The diet's emphasis on antioxidants, omega-3 fatty acids, and anti-inflammatory foods, such as fruits, vegetables, and fish, may help protect the brain from age-related damage and promote brain health.

Weight Management: The Mediterranean diet is not only effective for weight loss but also for weight management in women over 60. The diet's emphasis on whole, nutrient-dense foods and portion control helps promote satiety and reduce calorie intake, making it easier to maintain a healthy weight.

Bone Health: The Mediterranean diet is rich in calcium and vitamin D, both of which are essential for bone health and reducing the risk of osteoporosis in women over 60. Foods such as dairy products, leafy greens, nuts, and fish provide important nutrients that support bone strength and density.

Digestive Health: The Mediterranean diet is high in fiber, thanks to its emphasis on fruits, vegetables, whole grains, and legumes. Fiber promotes digestive health by preventing constipation, improving bowel regularity, and supporting a healthy gut microbiome.

Reduced Inflammation: The Mediterranean diet is naturally anti-inflammatory, thanks to its abundance of fruits, vegetables, nuts, seeds, and fatty fish, which are rich in antioxidants and omega-3 fatty acids. This can help reduce inflammation in the body, which is linked to chronic diseases such as heart disease, arthritis, and cancer.

Longevity: Studies have consistently shown that adherence to the Mediterranean diet is associated with a longer lifespan and a reduced risk of premature death from all causes. The diet's focus on whole, nutrient-rich foods and healthy lifestyle habits promotes overall health and well-being in women over 60, helping them live longer, healthier lives.

Principles of the Mediterranean Diet

The principles of the Mediterranean diet are rooted in the traditional dietary patterns of countries bordering the Mediterranean Sea, such as Greece, Italy, Spain, and Morocco. At its core, the Mediterranean diet emphasizes whole, minimally processed foods that are rich in nutrients and flavor. Key principles of the Mediterranean diet include: The majority of the diet consists of fruits, vegetables, whole grains, legumes, nuts, and seeds. These foods are high in fiber, vitamins, minerals, and antioxidants, which support overall health and well-being. Healthy Fats: Olive oil is the primary source of fat in the Mediterranean diet, used for cooking and dressing salads. Other sources of healthy fats include nuts, seeds, and fatty fish, which provide omega-3 fatty acids that are beneficial for heart health and brain function.

Moderate Consumption of Dairy and Poultry: Dairy products, such as cheese and yogurt, are consumed in moderation, while poultry is enjoyed occasionally. Red meat is limited, and processed meats are avoided.

Fresh Herbs and Spices: Herbs and spices are used liberally to add flavor to dishes, reducing the need for excess salt and unhealthy seasonings.

Enjoyment of Meals: Meals are enjoyed slowly and savored, often shared with family and friends. This encourages mindful eating and fosters a positive relationship with food.

Adaptations for Women Over 60

Adapting the Mediterranean diet for women over 60 involves tailoring the eating pattern to meet the unique nutritional needs and lifestyle considerations of this demographic. Some key adaptations include:

Increased Calcium and Vitamin D: Women over 60 are at higher risk for osteoporosis and bone fractures, so it's important to include plenty of calcium-rich foods, such as dairy products, leafy greens, and fortified foods. Vitamin D, which helps with calcium absorption, can be obtained from sources like fatty fish, eggs, and fortified foods.

Focus on Heart Health: As women age, the risk of heart disease increases. Emphasizing heart-healthy fats from sources like olive oil, nuts, seeds, and fatty fish can help maintain cardiovascular health. Limiting sodium intake and choosing whole, minimally processed foods can also support heart health.

Mindful Portion Control: Metabolism tends to slow down with age, so it's important for women over 60 to practice mindful portion control to maintain a healthy weight. Choosing nutrient-dense foods and avoiding excessive calorie-dense snacks can help support weight management.

Emphasis on Brain Health: Cognitive function may decline with age, so including foods rich in antioxidants, omega-3 fatty acids, and vitamins B6 and B12 can support brain health. This includes fruits, vegetables, fatty fish, nuts, seeds, and whole grains.

Hydration: Older adults may be at higher risk for dehydration, so staying hydrated is essential. Encouraging the consumption of water, herbal teas, and hydrating foods like fruits and vegetables can help prevent dehydration and support overall health in women over 60.

CHAPTER TWO

GETTING STARTED

Transitioning to the Mediterranean Diet

Transitioning to the Mediterranean diet can be an exciting and rewarding journey for women over 60. Here are some practical tips to help ease the transition and make the process enjoyable:

Start Gradually: Begin by incorporating small changes into your diet, such as adding an extra serving of vegetables to your meals or swapping out refined grains for whole grains. This gradual approach can help make the transition feel more manageable and sustainable.

Embrace Variety: Experiment with different foods and flavors to discover what you enjoy most about the Mediterranean diet. Try incorporating a wide variety of fruits, vegetables, whole grains, legumes, nuts, seeds, and seafood into your meals to keep things interesting and flavorful.

Plan Ahead: Take some time to plan your meals and snacks for the week ahead. This can help you make healthier choices and avoid reaching for convenience foods when you're short on time. Consider batch cooking and meal prepping to make healthy eating easier and more convenient.

Focus on Whole Foods: Choose whole, minimally processed foods whenever possible. These foods are rich in nutrients and flavor, and they can help support your overall health and well-being.

Listen to Your Body: Pay attention to how different foods make you feel and adjust your diet accordingly. Everyone's nutritional needs are unique, so it's important to listen to your body and eat in a way that makes you feel your best.

By taking a gradual and mindful approach to transitioning to the Mediterranean diet, women over 60 can enjoy the numerous health benefits of this delicious and nutritious eating pattern.

Stocking Your Pantry and Kitchen Essentials

Stocking your pantry and kitchen essentials is an essential step in getting started with the Mediterranean diet for women over 60. By having the right ingredients on hand, you can easily prepare delicious and nutritious meals that align with the principles of this eating pattern. Here are some key pantry staples and kitchen essentials to consider:

Olive Oil: Olive oil is a cornerstone of the Mediterranean diet, used for cooking, dressing salads, and adding flavor to dishes. Opt for extra virgin olive oil, which is the least processed and retains the most nutrients and flavor.

Whole Grains: Stock up on whole grains such as brown rice, quinoa, barley, bulgur, and whole wheat pasta. These grains are rich in fiber, vitamins, and minerals and can be used as a base for grain bowls, salads, and side dishes.

Legumes: Beans, lentils, and chickpeas are versatile and nutritious ingredients that are commonly used in Mediterranean cooking. They're rich in protein, fiber, and micronutrients and can be used in soups, stews, salads, and dips like hummus.

Canned Tomatoes: Canned tomatoes are a convenient pantry staple that can be used to make sauces, soups, and stews.

Look for varieties without added salt or sugar for a healthier option.

Herbs and Spices: Herbs and spices add flavor and depth to Mediterranean dishes without the need for excess salt or unhealthy seasonings. Stock up on staples like garlic, oregano, basil, thyme, rosemary, cumin, and paprika.

Nuts and Seeds: Almonds, walnuts, pistachios, and seeds like chia, flax, and sesame are rich in healthy fats, protein, and fiber. They can be enjoyed as snacks, added to salads, or used as toppings for yogurt and oatmeal.

Dried Fruit: Dried fruits like raisins, apricots, dates, and figs are sweet and nutritious additions to oatmeal, salads, and trail mix.

Seafood: Opt for canned or frozen seafood like tuna, salmon, sardines, and shrimp for convenient protein sources that can be added to salads, pasta dishes, and sandwiches.

By stocking your pantry and kitchen with these Mediterranean diet essentials, women over 60 can easily prepare delicious and nutritious meals that promote health and well-being.

Tips for Meal Planning and Preparation

Meal planning and preparation are key components of successfully adopting the Mediterranean diet for women over 60. Here are some helpful tips to streamline the process and ensure delicious and nutritious meals:

Plan Ahead: Set aside some time every week to organize your snacks and meals. Consider creating a weekly meal plan that includes a variety of Mediterranean-inspired dishes, such as salads, soups, grain bowls, and

seafood.

Batch Cooking: Consider batch-cooking staple ingredients like grains, beans, and proteins at the beginning of the week. This can help save time and make meal preparation easier throughout the week.

Use Leftovers Wisely: Repurpose leftovers into new meals to minimize food waste and save time in the kitchen. For example, leftover roasted vegetables can be added to salads or omelets, and leftover grilled chicken can be used in sandwiches or wraps.

Keep it Simple: Focus on simple, flavorful recipes that require minimal ingredients and preparation. Embrace the beauty of Mediterranean cuisine by letting fresh, seasonal ingredients shine.

Stock Up on Convenience Items: Invest in convenience items like pre-washed salad greens, frozen vegetables, and canned beans and tomatoes to make meal preparation easier and more convenient.

Embrace Meal Prep Tools: Invest in meal prep tools like a sharp knife, cutting board, vegetable peeler, and food storage containers to make meal preparation more efficient and enjoyable.

By incorporating these meal planning and preparation tips into your routine, women over 60 can easily embrace the Mediterranean diet and enjoy the numerous health benefits it offers.

Dietary Restrictions and Modifications

Adapting the Mediterranean diet to individual dietary restrictions and preferences is essential for women over 60 to fully enjoy the benefits of this eating pattern. Here are some strategies for navigating common dietary restrictions and making modifications:

Gluten-Free: For women with gluten intolerance or celiac disease, focus on naturally gluten-free grains like quinoa, rice, buckwheat, and corn. Choose gluten-free bread, pasta, and other grain products made from alternative flour like almond flour, coconut flour, or chickpea flour.

Dairy-Free: Substitute dairy products with non-dairy alternatives like almond milk, coconut yogurt, or cashew cheese. Look for calcium-fortified plant-based milk alternatives to ensure adequate calcium intake.

Vegetarian or Vegan: Incorporate plant-based sources of protein like beans, lentils, tofu, tempeh, and edamame into your meals. Include plenty of fruits, vegetables, whole grains, nuts, seeds, and plant-based fats like olive oil to ensure a well-balanced diet.

Low Sodium: Reduce sodium intake by using herbs, spices, citrus, and vinegar to flavor dishes instead of salt. Choose low-sodium canned goods and look for products labeled "no salt added" or "unsalted."

Low Carb: Focus on non-starchy vegetables, lean proteins, and healthy fats while limiting high-carb foods like bread, pasta, and sweets. Choose whole, minimally processed foods and include plenty of fiber-rich options like vegetables, fruits, nuts, and seeds.

Allergies: Avoid allergens by carefully reading ingredient labels and opting for allergen-free alternatives. Substitute ingredients as needed and consider experimenting with different recipes to find suitable alternatives.

CHAPTER THREE

Breakfast Recipes

Mediterranean Vegetable Frittata

Serving: One

Cooking Time: 25 minutes

Ingredients:
- 1/2 tablespoon olive oil
- 1/4 cup chopped red bell pepper
- 1/4 cup chopped zucchini
- 1/4 cup chopped cherry tomatoes
- 2 large eggs
- 2 tablespoons crumbled feta cheese
- 1 tablespoon chopped fresh parsley
- Salt and pepper to taste

Preparation:

1. Preheat the broiler.

2. In a small ovenproof nonstick skillet, heat the olive oil over medium heat. Add the bell pepper and zucchini and cook until softened about 3 minutes.

3. Add the cherry tomatoes and cook for 1 minute.

4. In a small bowl, whisk the eggs, then pour them over the vegetables in the skillet. Cook, lifting the edges to allow the uncooked eggs to flow underneath until the eggs are almost set, about 3 minutes.

5. Sprinkle the feta cheese over the top and place the skillet under the broiler. Broil until the eggs are set and the top is golden about 2 minutes.

6. Sprinkle with parsley, salt, and pepper. Slide the frittata onto a plate and serve.

Nutritional Value (Approximate):

Calories: 330

Protein: 19g

Fat: 24g

Carbohydrates: 11g

Fiber: 3g

Sugar: 6g

Sodium: 560mg

Cholesterol: 390mg

Blueberry Coconut Energy Bites

Serving: 10-12 bites

Cooking Time: 15 minutes

Ingredients:

- 1 cup old-fashioned oats
- 1/2 cup almond butter
- 1/4 cup honey
- 1/4 cup unsweetened shredded coconut
- 1/4 cup dried blueberries

•1/2 teaspoon vanilla extract

•A pinch of salt

Preparation:

1. In a large bowl, mix the oats, almond butter, honey, coconut, blueberries, vanilla extract, and salt until well combined.

2. Roll the mixture into 1-inch balls and place them on a parchment-lined baking sheet.

3. Refrigerate for at least 30 minutes before serving.

Nutritional Value (Approximate):

Calories: 100 per bite

Protein: 3g

Fat: 6g

Carbohydrates: 10g

Fiber: 2g

Sugar: 5g   Sodium: 25mg

Spinach and Feta Breakfast Wrap

Serving: One

Cooking Time: 10 minutes

Ingredients:

- 1 whole wheat tortilla
- 1/2 cup fresh spinach
- 2 large eggs, scrambled
- 2 tablespoons crumbled feta cheese
- Salt and pepper to taste

Preparation:

1. Place the tortilla on a plate and layer the fresh spinach on top.

2. Spoon the scrambled eggs onto the spinach.

3. Sprinkle the feta cheese over the eggs and season with salt and pepper.

4. Fold the sides of the tortilla over the eggs and roll it up into a wrap.

Nutritional Value (Approximate):

Calories: 350

Protein: 20g

Fat: 18g

Carbohydrates: 28g

Fiber: 5g

Sugar: 2g

Sodium: 600mg

Cholesterol: 390mg

Strawberry-Thyme Millet Bowl

Serving: One

Cooking Time: 20 minutes

Ingredients:

- 1/2 cup cooked millet
- 1/2 cup sliced strawberries
- 1 tablespoon honey
- 1/2 teaspoon fresh thyme leaves
- 2 tablespoons chopped walnuts
- 1/4 cup plain Greek yogurt

Preparation:

1. In a bowl, combine the cooked millet, sliced strawberries, honey, and fresh thyme leaves.

2. Top with chopped walnuts and a dollop of plain Greek yogurt.

Nutritional Value (Approximate):

Calories: 300

Protein: 9g

Fat: 12g

Carbohydrates: 40g

Fiber: 6g

Sugar: 12g

Sodium: 50mg

Cholesterol: 5mg

Orange Shakshuka

Serving: One

Cooking Time: 20 minutes

Ingredients:

- 1/2 tablespoon olive oil
- 1/4 cup chopped onion
- 1 clove garlic, minced
- 1/2 cup canned diced tomatoes
- 1/2 teaspoon paprika
- 1/4 teaspoon cumin
- 1/4 teaspoon cayenne pepper
- 2 large eggs
- 1/2 orange, segmented
- 1 tablespoon chopped fresh cilantro
- Salt and pepper to taste

Preparation:

1. Heat the olive oil in a small skillet over medium heat. Add the chopped onion and cook until softened about 3 minutes.

2. Add the minced garlic and cook for 1 minute.

3. Pour in the canned diced tomatoes and stir in the paprika, cumin, and cayenne pepper. Simmer for 5 minutes.

4. Make two wells in the tomato mixture and crack the eggs into them. Cover and cook until the egg whites are set but the yolks are still runny about 5 minutes.

5. Top with orange segments, chopped cilantro, salt, and pepper.

Nutritional Value (Approximate):

Calories: 320

Protein: 14g

Fat: 20g

Carbohydrates: 24g

Fiber: 6g

Sugar: 12g

Sodium: 400mg

Cholesterol: 370mg

Peach and Cherry Frozen Yogurt Bark

Serving: One

Cooking Time: 3 hours (including freezing time)

Ingredients:

- 1/2 cup plain Greek yogurt
- 1/4 cup sliced peaches
- 1/4 cup pitted cherries, halved
- 1 tablespoon honey

•1 tablespoon unsweetened shredded coconut

Preparation:

1. Line a small baking sheet with parchment paper.

2. Spread the Greek yogurt on the parchment paper into a 1/4-inch thick layer.

3. Arrange the sliced peaches and halved cherries on top of the yogurt.

4. Drizzle the honey over the fruit and yogurt, then sprinkle the unsweetened shredded coconut.

5. Freeze for at least 3 hours, then break into pieces and serve.

Nutritional Value (Approximate):

Calories: 150

Protein: 7g

Fat: 5g

Carbohydrates: 20g

Fiber: 3g

Sugar: 15g

Sodium: 30mg

Cholesterol: 5mg

Apple Walnut Muesli

Serving: One

Preparation Time: 10 minutes

Ingredients:
- 1/2 cup old-fashioned oats
- 1/2 cup unsweetened almond milk
- 1/2 apple, grated
- 2 tablespoons chopped walnuts
- 1 tablespoon honey
- 1/4 teaspoon ground cinnamon

Preparation:

1. In a bowl, combine the old-fashioned oats and unsweetened almond milk. Let it sit for 5 minutes.

2. Stir in the grated apple, chopped walnuts, honey, and ground cinnamon.

Nutritional Value (Approximate):

Calories: 320

Protein: 9g

Fat: 15g

Carbohydrates: 40g

Fiber: 8g

Sugar: 15g

Sodium: 80mg

Oat Chia Banana Muffins

Serving: 6 muffins

Cooking Time: 25 minutes

Ingredients:

- 1 cup old-fashioned oats

- 1/4 cup chia seeds
- 1/2 teaspoon baking powder
- 1/4 teaspoon baking soda
- 2 ripe bananas, mashed
- 1/4 cup honey
- 1/4 cup unsweetened applesauce
- 1 large egg
- 1/2 teaspoon vanilla extract

Preparation:

1. Preheat the oven to 350°F (175°C) and line a muffin tin with paper liners.

2. In a bowl, mix the old-fashioned oats, chia seeds, baking powder, and baking soda.

3. In another bowl, whisk the mashed bananas, honey, applesauce, egg, and vanilla extract.

4. Combine the wet and dry ingredients, then divide the batter among the muffin cups.

5. Bake for 20-25 minutes until a toothpick inserted into the center comes out clean.

CHAPTER FOUR

Lunch Recipes

Caprese Sandwich with Basil Pesto

Serving: One
Cooking Time: 10 minutes

Ingredients:
- 2 slices whole grain bread
- 2 slices fresh mozzarella cheese
- 1/2 cup sliced tomatoes
- 1 tablespoon basil pesto
- Salt and pepper to taste

Preparation:

1. Toast the bread slices.

2. Spread the basil pesto on one slice of bread.

3. Layer the fresh mozzarella cheese and sliced tomatoes on top of the pesto.

4. Season with salt and pepper, then top with the other slice of bread.

Nutritional Value (Approximate):

Calories: 400

Protein: 20g

Fat: 20g

Carbohydrates: 35g

Fiber: 6g

Sugar: 6g

Sodium: 600mg

Cholesterol: 45mg

Lentil Soup with Spinach and Lemon

Serving: One

Cooking Time: 30 minutes

Ingredients:
- 1/2 tablespoon olive oil
- 1/4 cup chopped onion
- 1 clove garlic, minced
- 1/2 cup dried green lentils
- 2 cups low-sodium vegetable broth
- 1/2 cup chopped fresh spinach
- 1/2 lemon, juiced
- Salt and pepper to taste

Preparation:

1. Heat the olive oil in a medium pot over medium heat. Add the chopped onion and cook until softened about 3 minutes.

2. Add the minced garlic and cook for 1 minute.

3. Add the dried green lentils and vegetable broth. Bring to a boil, then reduce the heat and simmer for 20-25 minutes until the lentils are tender.

4. Stir in the chopped fresh spinach and lemon juice. Season with salt and pepper.

Nutritional Value (Approximate):
Calories: 300
Protein: 18g
Fat: 5g
Carbohydrates: 45g
Fiber: 20g
Sugar: 5g
Sodium: 500mg
Cholesterol: 0mg

Piled-High Vegetable Pitas

Serving: One
Cooking Time: 15 minutes

Ingredients:

- 1 whole wheat pita
- 1/4 cup hummus
- 1/4 cup chopped cucumber
- 1/4 cup chopped red bell pepper
- 1/4 cup chopped cherry tomatoes
- 1/4 cup crumbled feta cheese
- Salt and pepper to taste

Preparation:

1. Cut the whole wheat pita in half to form two pockets.

2. Spread the hummus inside each pocket. Stuff the pockets with the chopped cucumber, red bell pepper, cherry tomatoes, and crumbled feta cheese.

3. Season with salt and pepper.

Nutritional Value (Approximate):

Calories: 350

Protein: 15g

Fat: 15g

Carbohydrates: 40g

Fiber: 8g

Sugar: 8g

Sodium: 700mg

Cholesterol: 25mg

Tomato & Avocado Cheese Sandwich

Serving: One

Preparation Time: 10 minutes

Ingredients:

• 2 slices whole grain bread

• 1/2 ripe avocado, sliced

• 1/2 medium tomato, sliced

• 2 slices of your favorite cheese

• 1 tablespoon olive oil

•Salt and pepper to taste

Preparation:

1. Place the cheese slices on one slice of bread.

2. Layer the avocado and tomato slices on top of the cheese.

3. Drizzle with olive oil and season with salt and pepper.

4. Top with the other slice of bread.

Nutritional Value (Approximate):
Calories: 420
Protein: 18g
Fat: 25g
Carbohydrates: 30g
Fiber: 12g

Sugar: 5g

Sodium: 550mg

Cholesterol: 60mg

Eggplant Pomodoro Pasta

Serving: One

Cooking Time: 30 minutes

Ingredients:
- 1 small eggplant, cubed
- 1/2 cup whole wheat spaghetti
- 1/2 cup marinara sauce
- 2 tablespoons grated Parmesan cheese
- 1 tablespoon chopped fresh basil
- 1 tablespoon olive oil
- 1 clove garlic, minced
- Salt and pepper to taste

Preparation:
1. Cook the whole wheat spaghetti according to the package instructions.

2. Meanwhile, heat the olive oil in a pan over medium heat. Add the minced garlic and cook for 1 minute.

3. Add the cubed eggplant and cook until softened, about 8-10 minutes.

4. Toss the cooked spaghetti with the marinara sauce and top with the cooked eggplant.

5. Sprinkle with grated Parmesan cheese, chopped fresh basil, salt, and pepper.

Nutritional Value (Approximate):
Calories: 380
Protein: 12g
Fat: 15g
Carbohydrates: 50g
Fiber: 12g
Sugar: 10g

Sodium: 700mg

Cholesterol: 10mg

White Bean & Veggies Salad

Serving: One

Preparation Time: 15 minutes

Ingredients:

- 1/2 cup cooked white beans
- 1/2 cup chopped cucumber
- 1/2 cup chopped red bell pepper
- 1/4 cup chopped red onion
- 2 tablespoons chopped fresh parsley
- 2 tablespoons extra virgin olive oil
- 1 tablespoon red wine vinegar
- Salt and pepper to taste

Preparation:

1. In a bowl, combine the white beans, chopped cucumber, red bell pepper, red onion, and fresh parsley.

2. Drizzle with extra virgin olive oil and red wine vinegar.

3. Season with salt and pepper, then toss to combine.

Nutritional Value (Approximate):

Calories: 320

Protein: 12g

Fat: 15g

Carbohydrates: 35g

Fiber: 10g

Sugar: 5g

Sodium: 300mg

Salmon-Stuffed Avocados

Serving: One

Preparation Time: 15 minutes

Ingredients:

- 1 ripe avocado, halved and pitted
- 1/2 cup cooked salmon, flaked
- 2 tablespoons plain Greek yogurt
- 1 tablespoon lemon juice
- 1 tablespoon chopped fresh dill
- Salt and pepper to taste

Preparation:

1. In a bowl, mix the flaked salmon, plain Greek yogurt, lemon juice, and chopped fresh dill.

2. Season with salt and pepper.

3. Divide the salmon mixture between the avocado halves.

Nutritional Value (Approximate):
Calories: 350

Protein: 25g

Fat: 20g

Carbohydrates: 20g

Fiber: 15g

Sugar: 2g

Sodium: 300mg   Cholesterol: 60mg

Caprese Stuffed Portobello Mushrooms

Serving: One

Cooking Time: 25 minutes

Ingredients:

•2 portobello mushrooms, stems removed

•1/2 cup cherry tomatoes, halved

•1/2 cup fresh mozzarella, diced

•2 tablespoons balsamic glaze

•2 tablespoons chopped fresh basil

•1 tablespoon olive oil

•Salt and pepper to taste

Preparation:

1. Preheat the oven to 400°F (200°C) and line a baking sheet with parchment paper.

2. Place the portobello mushrooms on the baking sheet, gill side up.
3. Drizzle with olive oil and season with salt and pepper.

4. Divide the cherry tomatoes and fresh mozzarella between the mushrooms.

5. Bake for 20 minutes until the cheese is melted and bubbly.

6. Drizzle with balsamic glaze and sprinkle with chopped fresh basil.

CHAPTER FIVE

Fish & Seafood

Tuna Burgers

Serving: One
Cooking Time: 15 minutes

Ingredients:
- 4 oz canned tuna, drained
- 1/4 cup whole wheat bread crumbs
- 1 tablespoon chopped red onion
- 1/2 teaspoon Dijon mustard
- 1/2 teaspoon lemon juice
- 1 teaspoon chopped fresh parsley
- Salt and pepper to taste
- 1 whole grain burger bun
- Lettuce and tomato for serving

Preparation:

1. In a bowl, mix the canned tuna, whole wheat bread crumbs, chopped red onion, Dijon mustard, lemon juice, chopped fresh parsley, salt, and pepper.

2. Form the mixture into a patty and cook in a non-stick skillet over medium heat for 3-4 minutes per side.

3. Serve the tuna patty on a whole grain burger bun with lettuce and tomato.

Nutritional Value (Approximate):
Calories: 350
Protein: 30g
Fat: 10g
Carbohydrates: 30g
Fiber: 6g
Sugar: 5g
Sodium: 600mg

Cholesterol: 30mg

Prawns with Mushroom

Serving: One

Cooking Time: 20 minutes

Ingredients:

- 6 large prawns, peeled and deveined
- 1 cup sliced mushrooms
- 1 clove garlic, minced
- 1 tablespoon olive oil
- 1/2 lemon, juiced
- 1 tablespoon chopped fresh parsley
- Salt and pepper to taste

Preparation:

1. Heat the olive oil in a pan over medium heat. Add the minced garlic and cook for 1 minute.

2. Add the sliced mushrooms and cook until softened about 5 minutes.

3. Add the prawns to the pan and cook for 2-3 minutes per side until pink and opaque.

4. Squeeze the lemon juice over the prawns and mushrooms, then sprinkle with chopped fresh parsley.

5. Season with salt and pepper.

Nutritional Value (Approximate):
Calories: 250
Protein: 25g
Fat: 10g
Carbohydrates: 10g
Fiber: 3g
Sugar: 3g
Sodium: 450mg
Cholesterol: 180mg

Chili Flounder Parcels

Serving: One

Cooking Time: 20 minutes

Ingredients:
- 1 flounder fillet
- 1/2 teaspoon chili powder
- 1/4 teaspoon ground cumin
- 1/4 teaspoon garlic powder
- 1/2 cup mixed bell peppers, julienned
- 1/4 cup red onion, thinly sliced
- 1/2 lemon, juiced
- 1 tablespoon chopped fresh cilantro
- Salt and pepper to taste

Preparation:

1. Preheat the oven to 375°F (190°C).

2. Place the flounder fillet on a piece of parchment paper.

3. Season the flounder with chili powder, ground cumin, garlic powder, salt, and pepper.

4. Top the flounder with the julienned bell peppers, sliced red onion, and chopped fresh cilantro.

5. Squeeze the lemon juice over the top, then fold the parchment paper to create a sealed parcel.

6. Bake for 15 minutes until the fish is cooked through.

Nutritional Value (Approximate):
Calories: 200
Protein: 25g
Fat: 5g
Carbohydrates: 10g
Fiber: 3g
Sugar: 3g

Sodium: 300mg

Cholesterol: 55mg

Dill Chutney Salmon

Serving: One

Cooking Time: 15 minutes

Ingredients:

- 1 salmon fillet
- 1 tablespoon chopped fresh dill
- 1 tablespoon chopped fresh parsley
- 1 tablespoon chopped red onion
- 1 tablespoon olive oil
- 1/2 lemon, juiced
- Salt and pepper to taste

Preparation:

1. Preheat the oven to 400°F (200°C).

2. Place the salmon fillet on a piece of foil.

3. In a bowl, mix the chopped fresh dill, chopped fresh parsley, chopped red onion, olive oil, lemon juice, salt, and pepper.

4. Spread the dill chutney mixture over the salmon.

5. Wrap the foil around the salmon to create a packet and bake for 12-15 minutes until the salmon is cooked through.

Nutritional Value (Approximate):

Calories: 300

Protein: 30g

Fat: 15g

Carbohydrates: 5g

Fiber: 1g

Sugar: 2g

Sodium: 400mg

Cholesterol: 70mg

Hazelnut Crested Sea Bass

Serving: One

Cooking Time: 20 minutes

Ingredients:
- 1 sea bass fillet
- 1/4 cup chopped hazelnuts
- 1/4 cup whole wheat bread crumbs
- 1 tablespoon chopped fresh parsley
- 1 tablespoon olive oil
- Salt and pepper to taste

Preparation:

1. Preheat the oven to 375°F (190°C).

2. In a bowl, mix the chopped hazelnuts, whole wheat bread crumbs, chopped fresh parsley, salt, and pepper.

3. Brush the sea bass fillet with olive oil, then coat with the hazelnut mixture.

4. Place the sea bass fillet on a baking sheet and bake for 15-18 minutes until the fish is cooked through.

Nutritional Value (Approximate):

Calories: 300

Protein: 30g

Fat: 15g

Carbohydrates: 10g

Fiber: 3g

Sugar: 2g

Sodium: 300mg

Cholesterol: 70mg

Marinara Mussels

Serving: One

Cooking Time: 15 minutes

Ingredients:

- 1 pound mussels, cleaned and debearded
- 1/2 cup marinara sauce
- 1/4 cup chopped fresh parsley
- 1/4 cup chopped red onion
- 1 clove garlic, minced
- 1 tablespoon olive oil
- Salt and pepper to taste

Preparation:

1. Heat the olive oil in a pan over medium heat. Add the minced garlic and cook for 1 minute.

2. Add the chopped red onion and cook until softened about 3 minutes.

3. Add the cleaned and debearded mussels to the pan and cook for 2-3 minutes until they start to open.

4. Pour the marinara sauce over the mussels and continue to cook until all the mussels have opened.

5. Sprinkle with chopped fresh parsley, salt, and pepper.

Nutritional Value (Approximate):

Calories: 300

Protein: 25g

Fat: 10g

Carbohydrates: 20g

Fiber: 3g

Sugar: 10g

Sodium: 800mg

Cholesterol: 50mg

Crispy Fish Sticks

Serving: One

Cooking Time: 20 minutes

Ingredients:

- 4 oz cod fillet
- 1/4 cup whole wheat bread crumbs
- 1/4 teaspoon garlic powder
- 1/4 teaspoon paprika
- 1/4 teaspoon dried oregano
- 1/4 teaspoon dried thyme
- 1 tablespoon olive oil
- Salt and pepper to taste

Preparation:

1. Preheat the oven to 400°F (200°C) and line a baking sheet with parchment paper.

2. Cut the cod fillet into strips.

3. In a bowl, mix the whole wheat bread crumbs, garlic powder, paprika, dried oregano, dried thyme, salt, and pepper.

4. Dip the cod strips into the olive oil, then coat with the bread crumb mixture.

5. Place the cod strips on the prepared baking sheet and bake for 15-18 minutes until the fish is cooked through and the coating is crispy.

Nutritional Value (Approximate):

Calories: 250

Protein: 20g

Fat: 10g

Carbohydrates: 20g

Fiber: 3g

Sugar: 2g

Sodium: 300mg

Cholesterol: 40mg

Roasted Cod with Cabbage

Serving: One

Cooking Time: 25 minutes

Ingredients:

- 1 cod filet (about 150g)
- 1 cup shredded cabbage
- 1/2 tablespoon olive oil
- 1/2 tablespoon lemon juice
- 1/2 teaspoon chopped fresh dill
- Salt and pepper to taste

Preparation:

1. Preheat the oven to 200°C.

2. Toss the shredded cabbage with olive oil, lemon juice, chopped fresh dill, salt, and pepper.

3. Place the seasoned cabbage on a baking sheet.

4. Season the cod fillet with salt and pepper, then place it on top of the cabbage.

5. Roast in the preheated oven for 15-18 minutes, or until the cod is cooked through and the cabbage is tender.

Nutritional Value (Approximate):

Calories: 200

Protein: 25g

Fat: 8g

Carbohydrates: 5g

Fiber: 3g

Sugar: 2g

Sodium: 300mg

Cholesterol: 60mg

CHAPTER SIX

Meat & Poultry

Herbed Beef Soup

Serving: 1
Preparation Time: 45 minutes

Ingredients:
- 3 oz. lean beef cubed
- 1/2 cup chopped onion
- 1/2 cup chopped carrots
- 1/2 cup chopped celery
- 1/2 cup chopped tomatoes
- 1/2 cup chopped zucchini
- 1/2 cup chopped spinach
- 1 tablespoon olive oil
- 1/2 teaspoon dried oregano
- 1/2 teaspoon dried thyme
- 1/2 teaspoon dried basil

- 1/2 teaspoon garlic powder
- 1/2 teaspoon salt
- 1/4 teaspoon black pepper
- 2 cups low-sodium beef broth

Preparation:

1. In a large pot, heat the olive oil over medium heat.

2. Add the beef and cook until browned on all sides.

3. Add the onion, carrots, and celery to the pot and cook until the vegetables are tender.

4. Add the tomatoes, zucchini, spinach, oregano, thyme, basil, garlic powder, salt, and black pepper to the pot and stir to combine.

5. Pour in the beef broth and bring to a boil.

6. Reduce the heat and simmer for 30 minutes until the beef is tender.

Approximate Nutritional Value:
Calories: 300
Protein: 25g
Fat: 10g
Carbohydrates: 25g
Fiber: 6g

Chicken Caprese

Serving: 1
Preparation Time: 30 minutes

Ingredients:
- 3 oz. cooked chicken breast
- 1/2 cup cherry tomatoes, halved
- 1/4 cup fresh mozzarella, diced
- 1/4 cup fresh basil leaves
- 1 tablespoon balsamic vinegar
- 1 tablespoon olive oil

•Salt and pepper to taste

Preparation:

1. In a bowl, combine the cherry tomatoes, mozzarella, basil, balsamic vinegar, olive oil, salt, and pepper.

2. Serve the chicken breast topped with the tomato mixture.

Approximate Nutritional Value:
Calories: 250
Protein: 25g
Fat: 15g
Carbohydrates: 5g
Fiber: 1g

Beef Kebabs with Onions and Peppers

Serving: 1

Preparation Time: 30 minutes

Ingredients:

- 3 oz. lean beef cubed
- 1/2 cup sliced onions
- 1/2 cup sliced bell peppers
- 1 tablespoon olive oil
- 1/2 teaspoon dried oregano
- 1/2 teaspoon dried thyme
- 1/2 teaspoon garlic powder
- Salt and pepper to taste

Preparation:

1. Preheat the grill to medium-high heat.

2. Thread the beef, onions, and bell peppers onto skewers.

3. In a small bowl, whisk together the olive oil, oregano, thyme, garlic powder, salt, and pepper.

4. Brush the skewers with the olive oil mixture.

5. Grill the skewers for 10-12 minutes until the beef is cooked to your liking.

Approximate Nutritional Value:
Calories: 250
Protein: 20g
Fat: 15g
Carbohydrates: 10g
Fiber: 2g

Chili Beef Stew

Serving: 1
Preparation Time: 2 hours

Ingredients:

- 3 oz. lean beef cubed
- 1/2 cup chopped onion
- 1/2 cup chopped carrots
- 1/2 cup chopped celery
- 1/2 cup chopped tomatoes
- 1/2 cup chopped zucchini
- 1/2 cup chopped spinach
- 1 tablespoon olive oil
- 1/2 teaspoon dried oregano
- 1/2 teaspoon dried thyme
- 1/2 teaspoon garlic powder
- 1/2 teaspoon salt
- 1/4 teaspoon black pepper
- 2 cups low-sodium beef broth

Preparation:

1. In a large pot, heat the olive oil over medium heat.

2. Add the beef and cook until browned on all sides.

3. Add the onion, carrots, and celery to the pot and cook until the vegetables are tender.

4. Add the tomatoes, zucchini, spinach, oregano, thyme, garlic powder, salt, and black pepper to the pot and stir to combine.

5. Pour in the beef broth and bring to a boil. Reduce the heat and simmer for 1-2 hours until the beef is tender.

Approximate Nutritional Value:
Calories: 300
Protein: 25g
Fat: 10g
Carbohydrates: 25g
Fiber: 6g

Zesty Turkey Breast

Serving: 1
Preparation Time: 30 minutes

Ingredients:
- 3 oz. turkey breast
- 1/2 cup cherry tomatoes, halved
- 1/4 cup fresh mozzarella, diced
- 1/4 cup fresh basil leaves
- 1 tablespoon balsamic vinegar
- 1 tablespoon olive oil
- Salt and pepper to taste

Preparation:

1. Preheat the oven to 375°F (190°C).

2. Place the turkey breast in a baking dish.

3. In a small bowl, whisk together the balsamic vinegar, olive oil, salt, and pepper.

4. Pour the mixture over the turkey breast.

5. Bake for 25-30 minutes until the turkey is cooked through.

6. Serve topped with cherry tomatoes, fresh mozzarella, and basil leaves.

Approximate Nutritional Value:
Calories: 250
Protein: 25g
Fat: 15g
Carbohydrates: 5g
Fiber: 1g

Chicken Souvlaki

Serving: 1
Preparation Time: 30 minutes

 Ingredients:
•3 oz. chicken breast, cubed

- 1/2 cup cherry tomatoes, halved
- 1/4 cup red onion, diced
- 1/4 cup cucumber, diced
- 1/4 cup Greek yogurt
- 1 tablespoon lemon juice
- 1 tablespoon olive oil
- 1/2 teaspoon dried oregano
- Salt and pepper to taste

Preparation:

1. Preheat the grill to medium-high heat.

2. Thread the chicken and cherry tomatoes onto skewers.

3. In a small bowl, whisk together the Greek yogurt, lemon juice, olive oil, oregano, salt, and pepper.

4. Grill the skewers for 10-12 minutes until the chicken is cooked through.

5. Serve with diced red onion, cucumber, and the Greek yogurt sauce.

Approximate Nutritional Value:
Calories: 250
Protein: 25g
Fat: 10g
Carbohydrates: 10g
Fiber: 2g

Green Veggie & Turkey

Serving: 1
Preparation Time: 20 minutes

Ingredients:
- 3 oz. turkey breast, sliced
- 1/2 cup green beans, trimmed
- 1/2 cup broccoli florets
- 1/2 cup zucchini, sliced
- 1/4 cup fresh parsley, chopped
- 1 tablespoon olive oil

•1 tablespoon lemon juice

•Salt and pepper to taste

Preparation:

1. In a large pot of boiling water, blanch the green beans, broccoli, and zucchini for 2-3 minutes until tender-crisp.

2. Drain the vegetables and transfer them to a large bowl.

3. Add the sliced turkey breast, fresh parsley, olive oil, lemon juice, salt, and pepper to the bowl and toss to combine.

Approximate Nutritional Value:

Calories: 250

Protein: 25g

Fat: 10g

Carbohydrates: 10g

Fiber: 4g

Spanish-Style Meatballs in Almond Sauce

Serving: 1

Cooking Time: 45 minutes

Ingredients:

- 3 oz. lean ground chicken or turkey
- 1/4 cup blanched almonds
- 1 slice bread
- 2 tablespoons olive oil
- 2 large cloves garlic, chopped
- 2/3 cups dry white wine
- 1 teaspoon freshly grated nutmeg
- Sea salt and fresh ground pepper to taste
- 1 cup unbleached all-purpose flour for coating meatballs

Preparation:

1. In a large bowl, combine the ground chicken or turkey, half of the chopped garlic,

nutmeg, salt, and pepper. Form the mixture into meatballs and coat them with flour.

2. Heat 1 tablespoon of olive oil in a skillet over medium heat. Add the meatballs and cook until browned on all sides. Remove and set aside.

3. In the same skillet, heat the remaining olive oil. Add the bread and almonds, and cook, stirring frequently, until they are golden brown. Add the remaining garlic and cook for an additional 30 seconds.

4. Pour in the wine and boil for 1 - 2 minutes. Use a spatula or wooden spoon to scrape up the bits on the bottom of the pan.

5. Pour the sauce mixture into the bowl of a food processor. Pour in the vegetable stock and blend the mixture until smooth.

6. Return the meatballs to the skillet and pour the almond sauce over them. Simmer for 10 - 15 minutes until the meatballs are cooked through.

Approximate Nutritional Value:

Calories: 350

Protein: 25g

Fat: 15g

Carbohydrates: 20g

Fiber: 3g

CHAPTER SEVEN

Sides, Soups & Salads

Hearty Veggie Slaw

Serving: 1
Preparation Time: 15 minutes

Ingredients:
- 1 cup shredded red cabbage
- 1/2 cup shredded carrots
- 1/4 cup chopped fresh parsley
- 1/4 cup chopped fresh mint
- 2 tablespoons extra virgin olive oil
- 1 tablespoon fresh lemon juice
- 1/2 teaspoon honey
- Salt and pepper to taste

Preparation:

1. In a large bowl, combine the shredded red cabbage, shredded carrots, chopped fresh parsley, and chopped fresh mint.

2. In a small bowl, whisk together the extra virgin olive oil, fresh lemon juice, honey, salt, and pepper.

3. Pour the dressing over the vegetable mixture and toss to combine.

Approximate Nutritional Value:

Calories: 150

Protein: 2g

Fat: 10g

Carbohydrates: 15g

Fiber: 6g

Simple Mushroom Barley Soup

Serving: 1

Preparation Time: 45 minutes

Ingredients:
- 1/2 cup pearl barley
- 2 cups vegetable broth
- 1 tablespoon olive oil
- 1/2 cup chopped onion
- 1/2 cup chopped carrots
- 1/2 cup chopped celery
- 1 cup sliced mushrooms
- 1/2 teaspoon dried thyme
- Salt and pepper to taste

Preparation:

1. In a large pot, heat the olive oil over medium heat.

2. Add the onion, carrots, and celery to the pot and cook until the vegetables are tender.

3. Add the sliced mushrooms, dried thyme, salt, and pepper to the pot and stir to combine.

4. Pour in the vegetable broth and bring to a boil.

5. Add the pearl barley to the pot and reduce the heat to low.

6. Simmer for 30-40 minutes until the barley is tender.

Approximate Nutritional Value:
Calories: 250
Protein: 5g
Fat: 5g
Carbohydrates: 45g
Fiber: 10g

Cucumber Gazpacho

Serving: 1

Preparation Time: 15 minutes

Ingredients:
- 1 large cucumber, peeled and chopped
- 1/2 cup chopped red bell pepper
- 1/2 cup chopped red onion
- 1/4 cup chopped fresh parsley
- 1/4 cup chopped fresh mint
- 2 tablespoons extra virgin olive oil
- 2 tablespoons red wine vinegar
- Salt and pepper to taste

Preparation:

1. In a blender or food processor, combine the chopped cucumber, red bell pepper, red onion, fresh parsley, and fresh mint.

2. Add the extra virgin olive oil, red wine vinegar, salt, and pepper to the blender or food processor.

3. Blend until smooth.

4. Chill the gazpacho in the refrigerator for at least 1 hour before serving.

Approximate Nutritional Value:
Calories: 200
Protein: 2g
Fat: 15g
Carbohydrates: 15g
Fiber: 4g

Pesto Ravioli Salad

Serving: 1
Preparation Time: 15 minutes

Ingredients:

- 1 cup cooked cheese ravioli
- 1/2 cup cherry tomatoes, halved
- 1/4 cup chopped fresh basil
- 1/4 cup chopped fresh parsley
- 2 tablespoons pesto sauce
- 1 tablespoon extra virgin olive oil
- Salt and pepper to taste

Preparation:

1. In a large bowl, combine the cooked cheese ravioli, cherry tomatoes, fresh basil, and fresh parsley.

2. In a small bowl, whisk together the pesto sauce, extra virgin olive oil, salt, and pepper.

3. Pour the dressing over the ravioli mixture and toss to combine.

Approximate Nutritional Value:

Calories: 400

Protein: 15g

Fat: 25g

Carbohydrates: 30g

Fiber: 4g

Vegetable Fagioli Soup

Serving: 1

Preparation Time: 45 minutes

Ingredients:

- 1/2 cup cooked white beans
- 2 cups vegetable broth
- 1 tablespoon olive oil
- 1/2 cup chopped onion
- 1/2 cup chopped carrots
- 1/2 cup chopped celery
- 1 cup chopped zucchini
- 1/2 teaspoon dried oregano
- Salt and pepper to taste

Preparation:

1. In a large pot, heat the olive oil over medium heat.

2. Add the onion, carrots, and celery to the pot and cook until the vegetables are tender.

3. Add the chopped zucchini, dried oregano, salt, and pepper to the pot and stir to combine.

4. Pour in the vegetable broth and bring to a boil.

5. Add the cooked white beans to the pot and reduce the heat to low.

6. Simmer for 30-40 minutes until the vegetables are tender.

Approximate Nutritional Value:

Calories: 250

Protein: 10g

Fat: 5g

Carbohydrates: 45g

Fiber: 10g

Turkish Leek and Potato Soup

Serving: 1

Preparation Time: 45 minutes

Ingredients:

- 1 large leek, chopped
- 1 large potato, peeled and chopped
- 2 cups vegetable broth
- 1 tablespoon olive oil
- 1/2 teaspoon dried thyme
- Salt and pepper to taste

Preparation:

1. In a large pot, heat the olive oil over medium heat.

2. Add the chopped leek to the pot and cook until tender.

3. Add the chopped potato, vegetable broth, dried thyme, salt, and pepper to the pot and stir to combine.

4. Bring the mixture to a boil, then reduce the heat to low.

5. Simmer for 30-40 minutes until the potato is tender.

6. Use an immersion blender to puree the soup until smooth.

Approximate Nutritional Value:

Calories: 200

Protein: 3g

Fat: 5g

Carbohydrates: 35g

Fiber: 5g

Herby Tzatziki Sauce

Serving: 1

Preparation Time: 10 minutes

Ingredients:

- 1/2 cup Greek yogurt
- 1/4 cup chopped fresh dill
- 1/4 cup chopped fresh mint
- 1/4 cup chopped cucumber
- 1 tablespoon extra virgin olive oil
- 1 tablespoon fresh lemon juice
- Salt and pepper to taste

Preparation:

1. In a small bowl, combine the Greek yogurt, chopped fresh dill, chopped fresh mint, chopped cucumber, extra virgin olive oil, fresh lemon juice, salt, and pepper.

2. Stir to combine.

3. Chill the tzatziki sauce in the refrigerator for at least 1 hour before serving.

Approximate Nutritional Value:

Calories: 150

Protein: 10g

Fat: 10g

Carbohydrates: 5g

Fiber: 1g

Cherry and Pine nuts Couscous

Serving: 1

Preparation Time: 15 minutes

Ingredients:

- 1/2 cup cooked couscous
- 1/4 cup dried cherries
- 1/4 cup pine nuts
- 1/4 cup chopped fresh parsley
- 1/4 cup chopped fresh mint
- 1 tablespoon extra virgin olive oil
- 1 tablespoon fresh lemon juice
- Salt and pepper to taste

Preparation:

1. In a large bowl, combine the cooked couscous, dried cherries, pine nuts, chopped fresh parsley, and chopped fresh mint.

2. In a small bowl, whisk together the extra virgin olive oil, fresh lemon juice, salt, and pepper.

3. Pour the dressing over the couscous mixture and toss to combine.

Approximate Nutritional Value:

Calories: 350

Protein: 10g

Fat: 15g

Carbohydrates: 45g

Fiber: 5g

CHAPTER EIGHT

Snacks & Appetizers

Mediterranean Pinwheels   Appetizer

Serving: 1

Preparation Time: 15 minutes

Ingredients:

- 1 whole wheat tortilla
- 2 tablespoons hummus
- 1/4 cup chopped fresh spinach
- 1/4 cup chopped roasted red peppers
- 1/4 cup crumbled feta cheese
- Salt and pepper to taste

Preparation:

1. Lay the whole wheat tortilla flat on a cutting board.

2. Spread the hummus evenly over the tortilla.

3. Sprinkle the chopped fresh spinach, chopped roasted red peppers, and crumbled feta cheese over the hummus.

4. Season with salt and pepper to taste.
Roll the tortilla tightly into a pinwheel shape.

5. Slice the pinwheel into bite-sized pieces.

Approximate Nutritional Value:
Calories: 200
Protein: 8g
Fat: 10g
Carbohydrates: 20g
Fiber: 4g

Savory Cauliflower Steaks

Serving: 1

Preparation Time: 30 minutes

Ingredients:

•1/2 head cauliflower, sliced into 1/2-inch steaks
•1 tablespoon olive oil
•1/2 teaspoon smoked paprika
•1/4 teaspoon garlic powder
•Salt and pepper to taste

Preparation:

1. Preheat the oven to 400°F (200°C).

2. Line a baking sheet with parchment paper.

3. In a small bowl, whisk together the olive oil, smoked paprika, garlic powder, salt, and pepper.

4. Brush the cauliflower steaks with the olive oil mixture on both sides.

5. Place the cauliflower steaks on the prepared baking sheet. Roast for 20-25 minutes, or until the cauliflower is tender and lightly browned.

Approximate Nutritional Value:

Calories: 150

Protein: 5g

Fat: 10g

Carbohydrates: 10g

Fiber: 5g

Whipped Feta Cheese Dip

Serving: 1

Preparation Time: 10 minutes

Ingredients:

- 1/2 cup crumbled feta cheese
- 1/4 cup plain Greek yogurt
- 1 tablespoon extra virgin olive oil
- 1 tablespoon fresh lemon juice
- 1/2 teaspoon dried oregano
- Salt and pepper to taste

Preparation:

1. In a food processor or blender, combine the crumbled feta cheese, plain Greek yogurt, extra virgin olive oil, fresh lemon juice, dried oregano, salt, and pepper.

2. Blend until smooth and creamy.

3. Serve with pita chips, sliced vegetables, or crackers.

Approximate Nutritional Value:

Calories: 200

Protein: 10g

Fat: 15g Carbohydrates: 5g

Hummus with Crudité

Serving: 1

Preparation Time: 10 minutes

Ingredients:

•1/4 cup hummus

•1/2 cup mixed vegetables (such as carrots, cucumbers, and cherry tomatoes)

•1 tablespoon extra virgin olive oil

•Salt and pepper to taste

Preparation:

1. Arrange the mixed vegetables on a plate.

2. Place the hummus in a small bowl and drizzle with extra virgin olive oil.

3. Season with salt and pepper to taste.

4. Serve the hummus with the mixed vegetables for dipping.

Approximate Nutritional Value:

Calories: 150

Protein: 5g

Fat: 10g

Carbohydrates: 10g

Fiber: 5g

Berry and Rhubarb Cobbler

Serving: 1

Preparation Time: 45 minutes

Ingredients:

•1/2 cup mixed berries (such as strawberries, blueberries, and raspberries)

•1/2 cup rhubarb, chopped

•1 tablespoon honey

•1/4 cup almond flour

- 1/4 cup rolled oats
- 1 tablespoon extra virgin olive oil
- 1/2 teaspoon ground cinnamon

Preparation:

1. Preheat the oven to 375°F (190°C).

2. In a small bowl, combine the mixed berries, chopped rhubarb, and honey.

3. In a separate bowl, combine the almond flour, rolled oats, extra virgin olive oil, and ground cinnamon.

4. Mix until the ingredients are well combined and crumbly.

5. Spoon the berry and rhubarb mixture into a small baking dish.

6. Sprinkle the almond flour and oat mixture over the top of the fruit.

7. Bake for 25-30 minutes, or until the topping is golden brown and the fruit is tender.

Approximate Nutritional Value:
Calories: 250
Protein: 5g
Fat: 15g
Carbohydrates: 25g
Fiber: 5g

Salmon Cucumber Rolls

Serving: 1
Preparation Time: 15 minutes

Ingredients:
•2 oz. smoked salmon
•1/2 cucumber, sliced into thin strips

•1 tablespoon plain Greek yogurt

•1/2 tablespoon fresh dill, chopped

•Salt and pepper to taste

Preparation:

1. In a small bowl, combine the plain Greek yogurt, fresh dill, salt, and pepper.

2. Lay the cucumber slices flat on a cutting board.

3. Spread a thin layer of the Greek yogurt mixture on each cucumber slice.

4. Place a strip of smoked salmon on top of each cucumber slice.

5. Roll the cucumber slices tightly around the smoked salmon. Secure each roll with a toothpick.

Approximate Nutritional Value:

Calories: 150

Protein: 15g

Fat: 5g

Carbohydrates: 5g

Fiber: 1g

Spiced Nuts Mix

Serving: 1

Preparation Time: 20 minutes

Ingredients:

- 1/4 cup mixed nuts (such as almonds, cashews, and walnuts)
- 1 tablespoon extra virgin olive oil
- 1/2 teaspoon ground cumin
- 1/2 teaspoon ground coriander
- 1/4 teaspoon ground cinnamon
- Salt and pepper to taste

Preparation:

1. Preheat the oven to 350°F (175°C).

2. In a small bowl, combine the mixed nuts, extra virgin olive oil, ground cumin, ground coriander, ground cinnamon, salt, and pepper.

3. Mix until the nuts are well coated with the spice mixture.

4. Spread the nuts out in a single layer on a baking sheet.

5. Bake for 10-15 minutes, or until the nuts are lightly toasted and fragrant.

Approximate Nutritional Value:

Calories: 200

Protein: 5g

Fat: 15g

Carbohydrates: 10g

Fiber: 2g

Vegetarian Mezze Platter

Serving: 1

Preparation Time: 15 minutes

Ingredients:
- 1/4 cup hummus
- 1/4 cup tzatziki sauce
- 1/4 cup marinated artichoke hearts
- 1/4 cup kalamata olives
- 1/4 cup cherry tomatoes
- 1/4 cup cucumber slices
- 1/4 cup feta cheese, crumbled
- 1/4 cup pita chips

Preparation:

1. Arrange the hummus, tzatziki sauce, marinated artichoke hearts, kalamata olives, cherry tomatoes, cucumber slices, and crumbled feta cheese on a large plate.

2. Serve with pita chips for dipping.

Approximate Nutritional Value:
Calories: 400
Protein: 15g
Fat: 25g
Carbohydrates: 30g
Fiber: 5g

Easy Spanakopita

Serving: 1
Preparation Time: 30 minutes

Ingredients:
- 1/2 cup frozen spinach, thawed and drained
- 1/4 cup crumbled feta cheese
- 1/4 cup ricotta cheese
- 1/4 cup chopped scallions
- 1/4 teaspoon dried dill
- Salt and pepper to taste
- 1 sheet of phyllo dough

• 1 tablespoon extra virgin olive oil

Preparation:

1. Preheat the oven to 375°F (190°C).

2. In a small bowl, combine the thawed and drained spinach, crumbled feta cheese, ricotta cheese, chopped scallions, dried dill, salt, and pepper.

3. Lay the phyllo dough flat on a cutting board. Brush the phyllo dough with extra virgin olive oil.

4. Spoon the spinach and cheese mixture onto the phyllo dough. Roll the phyllo dough tightly around the spinach and cheese mixture.

5. Brush the outside of the phyllo dough with extra virgin olive oil.

6. Bake for 20-25 minutes, or until the phyllo dough is golden brown and crispy.

Approximate Nutritional Value:

Calories: 300

Protein: 10g

Fat: 20g

Carbohydrates: 20g

Fiber: 2g

CHAPTER NINE

Dessert Recipes

Chocolate Olive Oil Cake

Serving: 1
Preparation Time: 1 hour

Ingredients:
- 1/4 cup extra virgin olive oil
- 1/4 cup honey
- 1/4 cup unsweetened cocoa powder
- 1/4 cup almond flour
- 1/4 teaspoon sea salt

Preparation:
1. Preheat the oven to 325°F (165°C).

2. In a bowl, whisk together the olive oil and honey.

3. Add the cocoa powder, almond flour, and sea salt. Mix until well combined.

4. Pour the batter into a greased baking dish.

5. Bake for 25-30 minutes, or until a toothpick inserted into the center comes out clean.

Approximate Nutritional Value:

Calories: 350

Protein: 5g

Fat: 25g

Carbohydrates: 30g

Fiber: 5g

Greek Yogurt Panna Cotta

Serving: 1

Preparation Time: 4 hours

Ingredients:

- 1/2 cup plain Greek yogurt
- 1/4 cup honey
- 1 teaspoon vanilla extract
- 1 teaspoon gelatin
- 2 tablespoons water

Preparation:

1. In a small bowl, sprinkle the gelatin over the water. Let it sit for 5 minutes.

2. In a saucepan, warm the Greek yogurt, honey, and vanilla extract over low heat.

3. Once the gelatin has softened, add it to the warm yogurt mixture. Stir until the gelatin has completely dissolved.

4. Pour the mixture into a serving dish. Refrigerate for at least 4 hours, or until set.

Approximate Nutritional Value:

Calories: 200

Protein: 15g

Fat: 5g

Carbohydrates: 20g

Fiber: 0g

Bruleed Ricotta

Serving: 1

Preparation Time: 10 minutes

Ingredients:

- 1/2 cup ricotta cheese
- 1 tablespoon honey
- 1/4 teaspoon vanilla extract
- 1 tablespoon turbinado sugar

Preparation:

1. In a small bowl, mix the ricotta cheese, honey, and vanilla extract.

2. Spoon the mixture into a ramekin.

3. Sprinkle the turbinado sugar over the top of the ricotta mixture.

4. Use a kitchen torch to brulee the sugar until it is caramelized and golden brown.

Approximate Nutritional Value:

Calories: 200

Protein: 10g

Fat: 10g

Carbohydrates: 15g

Fiber: 0g

Italian Carrot Cake (Torta di Carote)

Serving: 1

Preparation Time: 1 hour

Ingredients:

- 1/2 cup almond flour
- 1/4 cup all-purpose flour
- 1/4 cup honey
- 1/4 cup extra virgin olive oil
- 1/2 teaspoon baking powder
- 1/2 teaspoon ground cinnamon
- 1/4 teaspoon ground nutmeg
- 1/4 teaspoon sea salt
- 1/2 cup grated carrots

Preparation:

1. Preheat the oven to 350°F (175°C).

2. In a large bowl, whisk together the almond flour, all-purpose flour, honey, extra virgin olive oil, baking powder, ground cinnamon, ground nutmeg, and sea salt.

3. Fold in the grated carrots.

4. Pour the batter into a greased baking dish.

5. Bake for 25-30 minutes, or until a toothpick inserted into the center comes out clean.

Approximate Nutritional Value:

Calories: 350

Protein: 5g

Fat: 25g

Carbohydrates: 30g

Fiber: 5g

Blood Orange Olive Oil Cake

Serving: 1

Preparation Time: 1 hour

Ingredients:

- 1/4 cup extra virgin olive oil
- 1/4 cup honey
- 1/4 cup almond flour
- 1/4 cup all-purpose flour
- 1/4 teaspoon baking powder

•1/4 teaspoon sea salt

•1/4 cup blood orange juice

•1 tablespoon blood orange zest

Preparation:

1. Preheat the oven to 325°F (165°C).

2. In a large bowl, whisk together the olive oil and honey.

3. Add the almond flour, all-purpose flour, baking powder, and sea salt. Mix until well combined.

4. Stir in the blood orange juice and blood orange zest.

5. Pour the batter into a greased baking dish.

6. Bake for 25-30 minutes, or until a toothpick inserted into the center comes out clean.

Approximate Nutritional Value:

Calories: 350

Protein: 5g

Fat: 25g

Carbohydrates: 30g

Fiber: 5g

Almond and Orange Biscotti

Serving: 1

Preparation Time: 1 hour

Ingredients:
- 1/2 cup almond flour
- 1/4 cup all-purpose flour
- 1/4 cup honey
- 1/4 cup extra virgin olive oil
- 1/4 teaspoon baking powder
- 1/4 teaspoon sea salt
- 1/4 cup slivered almonds
- 1 tablespoon orange zest

Preparation:

1. Preheat the oven to 325°F (165°C).

2. In a large bowl, whisk together the almond flour, all-purpose flour, honey, extra virgin olive oil, baking powder, and sea salt.

3. Fold in the slivered almonds and orange zest. Form the dough into a log shape on a baking sheet.

4. Bake for 25-30 minutes, or until lightly golden brown. Remove from the oven and let it cool for 10 minutes.

5. Slice the log into biscotti shapes. Place the biscotti back on the baking sheet and bake for an additional 10-15 minutes, or until crispy.

7-DAY MEAL PLAN

Day 1

Breakfast: Blueberry Coconut Energy Bites

Lunch: Lentil Soup with Spinach and Lemon

Dinner: Tuna Burgers with Hearty Veggie Slaw

Day 2

Breakfast: Spinach and Feta Breakfast Wrap

Lunch: Caprese Sandwich with Basil Pesto

Dinner: Chicken Souvlaki with Cherry and Pine nuts Couscous

Day 3

Breakfast: Strawberry-Thyme Millet Bowl

Lunch: Piled-High Vegetable Pitas

Dinner: Chili Beef Stew with Simple Mushroom Barley Soup

Day 4

Breakfast: Orange Shakshuka
Lunch: Eggplant Pomodoro Pasta
Dinner: Zesty Turkey Breast with Herby Tzatziki Sauce

Day 5

Breakfast: Peach and Cherry Frozen Yogurt Bark
Lunch: White Bean & Veggies Salad
Dinner: Beef Kebabs with onions and pepper with Cucumber Gazpacho

Day 6

Breakfast: Apple Walnut Muesli
Lunch: Salmon-Stuffed Avocados

Dinner: Spanish-Style Meatball with Almond Sauce with Turkish Leek and Potato Soup

Day 7

Breakfast: Oat Chia Banana Muffins

Lunch: Caprese Stuffed Portobello Mushrooms

Dinner: Roasted Cod with Cabbage with Pesto Ravioli Salad

Each day includes a variety of proteins, vegetables, fruits, grains, and dairy, ensuring a well-balanced diet throughout the week. Adjust portion sizes as needed based on individual dietary needs and preferences. Enjoy your meals!

CONCLUSION

In conclusion, this Mediterranean Diet Cookbook for women over 60 offers a diverse range of flavorful and nutritious recipes designed to support overall health and well-being. With an emphasis on fresh fruits and vegetables, whole grains, lean proteins, and healthy fats, this diet provides essential nutrients while promoting heart health, cognitive function, and longevity.

The recipes included in this cookbook draw inspiration from the rich culinary traditions of the Mediterranean region, known for its emphasis on wholesome ingredients and simple yet delicious flavors. From vibrant salads and hearty soups to mouthwatering seafood and indulgent desserts, there is something for every palate and occasion.

Beyond just delicious meals, the Mediterranean diet has been extensively researched and shown to offer numerous health benefits. Studies have linked this dietary pattern to reduced risk of chronic diseases such as cardiovascular disease, diabetes, and certain types of cancer. Additionally, the inclusion of antioxidant-rich foods like fruits, vegetables, and olive oil may help to protect against age-related cognitive decline and promote brain health.

As women over 60 embark on their journey towards better health and vitality, adopting and adapting to the Mediterranean diet can be a powerful step forward. Not only does this dietary approach offer the potential for physical benefits, but it also celebrates the joy of eating and nourishing the body with wholesome, delicious foods. By embracing the Mediterranean diet, women can cultivate a sustainable and enjoyable way of eating that supports their overall health and well-being for years to come. So why not embark on this culinary adventure and savor the flavors of the Mediterranean while reaping the rewards of a healthier lifestyle? Your body and taste buds will thank you!

Made in the USA
Monee, IL
13 September 2024

65633195R00077